DELIVERY DRIVERS

by Meg Gaertner

Cody Koala

An Imprint of Pop!
popbooksonline.com

abdopublishing.com

Published by Pop!, a division of ABDO, PO Box 398166, Minneapolis, Minnesota 55439. Copyright © 2019 by POP, LLC. International copyrights reserved in all countries. No part of this book may be reproduced in any form without written permission from the publisher. Pop!™ is a trademark and logo of POP, LLC.

Printed in the United States of America, North Mankato, Minnesota

042018
092018

Cover Photo: Shutterstock Images
Interior Photos: Shutterstock Images, 1, 10, 15, 16, 19 (bottom left), 19 (bottom right); iStockphoto, 5, 6, 9, 13, 17, 19 (top), 20
Editor: Charly Haley
Series Designer: Laura Mitchell

Library of Congress Control Number: 2017963074

Publisher's Cataloging-in-Publication Data

Names: Gaertner, Meg, author.
Title: Delivery drivers / by Meg Gaertner.
Description: Minneapolis, Minnesota : Pop!, 2019. | Series: Community workers | Includes online resources and index.
Identifiers: ISBN 9781532160080 (lib.bdg.) | ISBN 9781532161209 (ebook) |
Subjects: LCSH: Truck drivers--Juvenile literature. | Truck driving--Juvenile literature. | Delivery services--Juvenile literature. | Occupations--Careers--Jobs--Juvenile literature. | Community life--Juvenile literature.
Classification: DDC 388.324--dc23

Hello! My name is

Cody Koala

Pop open this book and you'll find QR codes like this one, loaded with information, so you can learn even more!

Scan this code* and others like it while you read, or visit the website below to make this book pop.

popbooksonline.com/delivery-drivers

*Scanning QR codes requires a web-enabled smart device with a QR code reader app and a camera.

Table of Contents

A Day in the Life

A **postal worker** picks up letters and packages from the post office. He drives through neighborhoods and brings people their mail.

Watch a video here!

Postal workers are one type of **delivery** driver. Delivery drivers bring items from one place to another.

The Work

Food delivery drivers
bring food from stores or
restaurants to homes nearby.
People order this food over
the phone or online.

Learn more here!

Truck drivers bring items
from one state to another.

Sometimes they drive across the whole country. They often drop off items at businesses or factories.

Truck drivers drive large trucks called semitrucks.

Some packages go through **distribution centers** instead of post offices. Package delivery drivers pick up these items. They bring them to **local** homes or offices.

Some delivery drivers deliver flowers or newspapers.

Chapter 3

Tools for Delivery Drivers

Many delivery drivers have **GPS**, or the global positioning system, on their smartphones or in their cars or trucks.

Learn more here!

GPS tracks a driver's location and gives them directions. This helps drivers bring deliveries to the right places.

Drivers can use a **dolly** to lift very heavy boxes. A dolly is a type of cart on wheels. Delivery drivers roll packages on the dolly instead of carrying them.

Chapter 4

Helping the Community

Delivery drivers help people who cannot leave their homes. People can buy something online. It will be brought straight to their homes.

Complete an activity here!

Delivery drivers bring

letters, packages, and items

to where they need to go.

Making Connections

Text-to-Self

Have you ever seen a delivery driver? What did he or she deliver? Would you ever want to be a delivery driver?

Text-to-Text

Have you read other books about community workers? How are their jobs different from a delivery driver's?

Text-to-World

Why do you think it is important to have delivery drivers? What might the world be like without them?

Glossary

delivery – a package brought by someone.

distribution center – a place where people sort through packages and send them out on delivery.

dolly – a tool used to lift heavy objects and move them on wheels.

GPS – a tool used to tell people where they are and how to get where they're going.

local – in the same neighborhood or community.

postal worker – a person who brings people their mail.

Index

Online Resources

popbooksonline.com

Thanks for reading this Cody Koala book!

Scan this code* and others like it in this book, or visit the website below to make this book pop!

popbooksonline.com/delivery-drivers

*Scanning QR codes requires a web-enabled smart device with a QR code reader app and a camera.